THIS IS NOT COOL

Volume II

Legal Lessons for Youth
&
Their Parents

THIS IS NOT COOL

Volume II

Legal Lessons for Youth
&
Their Parents

Clara Hunter King, Esq.
Yvonne Hawks, Esq.
Janine Brooks-Collier, PI
Betty Williams-Kirby, Esq.
Lawanda Jean O'Bannon, Esq.

MILLIGAN BOOKS **BOOKS** CALIFORNIA

Printed and Bound in the United States of America
Published and Distributed by:
Milligan Books, Inc.

Cover Layout by Kevin Allen
Formatting by Caldonia Joyce

First Printing, March 2007
10987654321

ISBN: 978-0-9792016-2-2

Milligan Books
1425 W. Manchester Blvd., Suite C
Los Angeles, CA 90047

www.milliganbooks.com
drrosie@aol.com
(323) 750-3592

DEDICATION

This book is dedicated to all the people who encouraged us to do something, rather than just talk, about the number of young men entering the criminal justice system. To all parents who are beginning to lose hope, may your hope be restored. Help is on the way.

ACKNOWLEDGEMENT

We would like to thank Dr. Rosie Milligan, our publisher, who helped us pull it all together.

INTRODUCTION

<u>This Is Not Cool</u> is a series of short stories written by members of WATCHDOGS FOR JUSTICE, a Georgia non-profit organization formed for the purpose of reducing the number of young people, especially young Black males, in jails and prisons. The stories are based on actual cases handled by the writers and are intended to show how easily one can get caught up in the criminal justice system. The authors conduct seminars in schools, libraries, churches, homeless shelters, and any other place they can find a group of young people willing to listen. On every occasion they endeavor to impress upon them the time to *"Stop And Ask Questions," "The Time To Walk Away,"* and *"The Time to Run And Not Look Back."* They open and close each seminar by reminding the youngsters of its purpose: to provide them with the information they need to *"Stay Out Of Prison."*

TABLE OF CONTENTS

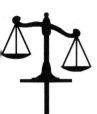

CHAPTER

1

Remember

The Night

Clara Hunter King

It was the day after Thanksgiving and Michael was trying to keep the shelves stocked at Handy Mart. He wondered where all the people came from. The customers seemed to have gone mad—they pushed each other and practically grabbed merchandise out of each other's hand. "Hello, big boy," said the young lady who was standing so close to him that he could feel her breath on his face when he turned around.

"Hello," he said. "How may I help you?"

"I'm Shayla. How would you like to come by my house tonight? My parents are on vacation, and I'll be home alone ... and lonely for the company of a handsome playboy like you."

Michael felt like an idiot, but he couldn't think of anything to say. "Eh ...," he began.

"Here's my address," she said as she handed him a piece of paper with her name, address, and phone number. Then she stepped back so that he could get a better look at her. She turned around slowly as if modeling the outfit she was wearing.

Michael stood there staring with his mouth open. He was in shock. He had never encountered a girl so bold before, and she *was* beautiful. She looked like she was melted and poured into that red dress. Quickly, he looked around to see if anyone was watching.

"What time?" he asked.

"The sooner the better. What time do you get off?"

"Six-thirty."

"Then seven-thirty should be good. That will give you time to pick up some wine on the way, and I'll have dinner ready."

"Okay," Michael said. "Seven-thirty it is."

The remainder of the day passed too slowly for Michael. He had his friend check out the directions to her house on the computer. He was looking forward to an evening of fun with his beautiful new friend. He was supposed to take the car home to his mom, but he called her and told her he had to work late.

"What time will you get home?" his mom asked.

"I'm not sure," he said. "This is a record-breaking year for shopping. The people are going crazy. I can't keep the shelves stocked fast enough. I may be here until midnight since we won't close until the last shopper has been taken care of."

"Well, okay," his mom answered. "I guess it can't be helped. I'll go buy groceries tomorrow."

"Thanks, Mom, I'll make it up to you."

At six-thirty, Michael practically ran from the store. He jumped in the car and headed towards Shayla's house, punching in a CD and singing along with the rappers as he drove. He stopped the car in front of the house for just a second, and then decided to drive right up in the driveway. After all, it would only be the two of them. He was glad he had told his mom he would be late. That way, she wouldn't wait up for him. He didn't have to be in a hurry.

Michael was just a wee bit nervous as he approached the door. "What if her parents really are home?" he asked himself. He decided there was only one way to find out. He rang the doorbell and waited. Shayla opened the door and smiled at him. "Come in," she said, as she stepped back to allow him to get a good look at her in her red short shorts and halter top.

Michael just stood there for a few seconds, taking it all in, then he quickly looked around to see if any of the neighbors were watching. Satisfied they weren't, he rushed in and closed the door and handed her the bottle of wine. "You may want to put that on some ice," he said, trying to act as if he drank wine every day.

"I have Granny's fried chicken and French fries. You didn't want a salad, did you?"

"No," he said. "Why mess up fried chicken and French fries with a salad? I didn't know they had French fries at Granny's." He looked around. The house was huge and nice.

15

"The fries came from Burger Hut," she replied as she moved up close to Michael and planted a soft kiss on his lips.

"Nice pad you got here."

"My parents are rich."

"I can tell." Michael felt way out of his league. He didn't know people like this—a girl with rich parents and more boldness than he had ever encountered in a female before.

They ate the chicken and French fries in the den as they listened to the latest rap music. After dinner, they drank the wine. Then Shayla stood and began to dance.

"Come on, playboy, we're going to have a good time tonight."

Michael stood and danced with her. He was trying to get used to her boldness. As she danced, she began to take off her clothes. Michael looked around; he was a little uncomfortable undressing with all the lights on.

"Hey, why don't we turn some of these light out?"

"This wouldn't happen to be your first time with a woman, would it, playboy?" Shayla teased as she continued to dance and step out of her clothes. Once she began to step out of her panties—the last item remaining—Michael moved over to the lamp and turned out the light. He looked at the blinds, hoping no one could see into the house. Shayla took him by the hand and led him into her bedroom. Michael had never seen a bedroom like that before—and he had never met a girl like Shayla before either.

When Michael awoke three hours later, he remembered that he had to get home with his mom's car. He had intended to sneak out, but decided to awaken Shayla because he wasn't sure if the alarm was on. Shayla was in a bad mood and practically threw him out. Michael was glad to be going home.

He felt guilty when he arrived home and realized that his mom had waited up for him. "Well, did you sell everything in the store?" she asked.

"Almost," Michael lied. "Mom, I hope you never go shopping the Friday after Thanksgiving. People lose all sense of decency and courtesy. The sales caused them to lose their mind. I saw little old ladies grabbing and snatching stuff out of each other's hands. It was like a madhouse, kind of like being at a movie."

Michael was busy stocking shelves when he looked up from his work and saw the manager and two policemen, one big and one small, walking in his direction. He was a little surprised when they walked right up to him and began to ask questions.

"Are you Michael Lowery?"

"Yes," Michael said. His mind was racing. He wondered what the police could possibly want to discuss with him.

"Would you come with us to the manager's office? We want to ask you a few questions." As soon as they were in the office, the questions began.

"Do you know a young lady by the name of Shayla Grimes?"

"No," Michael said. "I mean, I don't *really* know her. I met her here at the store a couple of days ago." His heart felt like someone had reached inside his chest and cupped it in their hands.

"Did you go to her house?" the big officer asked.

"Yes," Michael said. He turned to look at the manager, but he had already stepped out of the office and was pretending to look at the appliances that were on sale.

"Well, yes," Michael said as he laughed nervously. He did not like where this was going.

"Did you have sex with her?"

"Well ... yes, I did, but it was *her* idea. She came into the store during the big sale the day after Thanksgiving and invited me to her house, gave me her phone number and address. I thought we were just going to listen to music and watch TV. The sex was her idea."

"You are under arrest for statutory rape, and I must tell you that anything you say can and will be used against you in a court of law. You have—"

"But it was consensual," Michael insisted. "The whole thing was *her* idea."

"It doesn't matter. She is only 14 years old, and the law says she can't consent. You have the right to remain silent. You have the right to an attorney. If you can't afford one, one will be appointed—"

"Fourteen?!" Michael was almost screaming. "She told me she was 18, and it was *her* idea; all of it was her idea."

"It doesn't matter whose idea it was. She is only 14, and you are facing up to 20 years in prison." The policeman was reaching for Michael's hands as he moved the handcuffs forward. Michael wanted to cry. He knew what Shayla had in mind when she invited him to her home. He just didn't know she was only 14 and that he could possibly get 20 years in prison.

Shalya's parents were angry; Michael's mom was devastated. Michael learned that a neighbor had peeked in the window when he saw the car parked in the driveway because he knew the Grimes were out of town and Shayla was supposed to be staying with a friend. He had seen Michael and Shayla dancing, and later saw the lights turned off although he could still hear music. He called her parents and told them. Shayla readily admitted that she had had sex with Michael. She claimed that he talked her into it. She told how he had brought wine, and they drunk until they were tipsy.

Michael was so sick and angry with himself when he stood in court. Her parents were there, giving him hateful glances. His mom cried silently through the whole proceeding.

When he heard the 10-year sentence, he thought he would faint. But somehow his legs began to move as the deputy dragged him from the courtroom. He could not even turn his head to look back at his mom. He wanted to—God knows he wanted to—but his neck would not respond to his brain. He wondered if that was what was meant by the words "brain dead."

Prison was worse than he could have imagined. His cellmate was a 40-year-old idiot. *How can they put a 19 year old in a cell with a grown man?* Michael wondered.

He was sad every day. He was scared every day. He was homesick every day. Somehow he knew he could not maintain his sanity unless he did something differently. He decided to go to church. He was not interested in God, he just wanted to get out of his cell for a few hours on Sunday. So he began to look forward to Sundays. It was the only day that brought him a little joy. He concluded that his life would be different when his feet hit the ground again in the real world. The first thing he planned to do is learn something about the law. No one ever told him—and he never knew—that under Georgia law, he could be sentenced to up to 20 years in prison for having sex with a girl if she was under 16 and at least 3 years younger than himself. He also didn't know that a 14 year old could look so grown up.

There was something about what the preacher said while Michael was at church one Sunday that made him think that somehow, he could keep going, one day at a time. He had no other choice. So he began to take it one day at a time. He was still sad every day, he was still scared every day, and still homesick every day. He didn't want a calendar; he didn't want to keep track of time. He just knew at the end of each day that he had one less day left to serve. And somehow, that made him feel that he had accomplished something positive because—he had made it through another day.

MORAL LESSON

Michael learned too late that looks can be deceiving. If he had taken the time to get to know Shayla and meet her parents, he would have discovered that she was only 14. In the end, he paid a heavy price for a one-night stand. He learned the hard way that ignorance of the law is no excuse, and boldness and aggression in a young woman is not a true indication of maturity. Because Shayla was under 16 and Michael was at least 3 years older than she was, he was guilty of statutory rape, even though she initiated the contact. Remember, when it comes to sex with a person under 16, age is the most important factor in determining if you committed a crime.

CHAPTER
2

Whose Bag is That?

Clara Hunter King

aura was surprised when the officers, brandishing shiny badges, stopped her and Greg and asked to see their identification. She began searching for her driver's license and realized it was not in her wallet. She panicked. She could not find the license. She dumped everything out of her purse. It was not there. Then she remembered that she had stuffed it in the side flap of her purse after showing it at all the security checkpoints. She breathed a sigh of relief as she retrieved the license and handed it to the officer.

"Where are you going?" the officer asked, as he matched the names on the drivers' licenses to the names on the luggage. The second officer stood by and quietly observed.

"Miami," they said in unison. Laura was holding her eight-month-old baby.

"You mind stepping into that room over there? We want to ask you some questions."

"No, but is something wrong?" Laura asked as they walked towards the room.

"We hope not. Just checking." The officers didn't tell Laura that they were stopped because they had both purchased a one-way ticket using cash and were headed to a city high in drug trafficking.

"Did anyone ask you to carry any merchandise on the plane for them?"

"No," Greg and Laura answered.

"Are you carrying anything that belongs to someone else?" the officer asked as they took their seats at the table.

"No," Greg said as he began to slide the baby bag towards Laura.

"Whose bag is that?" the officer asked.

"Mine," Laura said as she reached out and picked up the bag.

"We have a drug dog that we want to check your luggage. If everything is okay, we'll be on our way. You don't mind, do you?"

"No," Laura and Greg replied in unison.

When the drug dog came in, he did not bark at Laura's or Greg's luggage, but he barked at Laura's baby bag that Greg had been carrying. When the officer opened the baby bag, he found a plastic bag with heroin. Laura was shocked. She turned and looked at Greg. "You had to have put that in my bag. Why?"

"Lady, I didn't put anything in your bag. I only helped you carry the bag because you had the baby. Don't try to blame that on me."

"Aren't you two traveling together?" the officer asked.

"No," Greg said. "We met at the airport. I offered to help her with the bags because she was carrying a baby and seemed to be struggling. I never met her before today."

"You are both under arrest for drug trafficking. You have the right to remain silent. Anything you say can and will be used against you in a court of law. You have the right to have an attorney represent you. If you can't afford one, one will be appointed for you. Do you understand your rights?" the officer asked.

"Yes, I understand my rights," said Laura. "And I did not have any drugs in my bag when he offered to carry it. I don't do drugs, and I have never had any drugs. It has to belong to him."

"We'll let the court sort it out. Put your hands behind you, please," the officer said to Greg. "We'll call Children Services to get the baby. You can stay here until they arrive," he told Laura.

"Officer, please," Laura implored, "those are not my drugs. I haven't done anything wrong."

The officer felt a little sorry for Laura, but the drugs were in her bag. It was not his call. "Like I said, let the court sort it out. We can't make that call."

By the time the Children Services worker arrived, the baby was screaming and Laura thought she was going to die. The more upset Laura became, the more the baby screamed. Laura was crying as she provided information about her mother and the phone number. The baby was kicking, screaming, and reaching for Laura as the worker took her away.

Greg had befriended Laura in Denver as they waited for the plane to Atlanta. He offered to help carry her bags. They sat side by side in the waiting area, and he seemed very friendly. When he went to buy himself a sandwich, he bought one for Laura. When they arrived in Atlanta, he continued to carry her bag as they walked to the waiting area for the flight out of Atlanta. They had a 45-minute layover, and Greg spent the entire time with Laura. He told jokes and offered to hold the baby, but she wouldn't let him because the baby wasn't feeling well. Laura could see the whole picture now. He had deliberately passed the bag back to her when the search began. She began to weep when she realized that he had offered to help her carry her bag and was so attentive to her because he wanted to plant his drugs in her baby's bag. Now she was separated from her baby for God only knows how long.

"My baby, my little baby," she wailed as the tears rolled down her face. She was filled with rage and desperation and humiliation as she was taken away in handcuffs for a crime she did not commit. *It's a dream, a nightmare,* she thought to herself. *This can't be happening. It just can't be.* Somehow her feet obeyed her command to walk as the officer led her to the vehicle that would take her to jail. It was the saddest day of her life.

After Laura was booked and fingerprinted, she was given the opportunity to make a phone call. She called her mother. She hoped to reach her mother before the Children Services worker did. Her mother was devastated. Laura asked her mother to notify her sister in Miami that she would not be coming for a visit after all. Her mother did not have the money to come to Atlanta. They had all put their money together to pay Laura's fare to visit her sister, who had just been diagnosed with breast cancer. Laura felt that her whole family would be wiped out. She did not see how they could survive this onslaught. Her mother sounded so pitiful. Laura knew that the only reason she didn't die while talking with her mother was because she couldn't leave her baby. She had to find a way to get her baby back. As Laura sat on her bunk, she tried to pray. She couldn't think of anything to say. Her mind had stopped working, the pain was too deep. She ignored all the other inmates and cried herself to sleep.

The charge against Greg was dropped. There was no evidence that he had any knowledge of the drugs. He signed a written statement that Laura had befriended him and asked him to help her carry the bag because her baby wasn't feeling well. When the investigator talked with Laura, she admitted that the baby wasn't feeling well. So Greg walked away, and Laura was left to face the charge alone.

When Laura learned that the penalty for trafficking in heroin was 25 years, she was beside herself with grief. "Those were not my drugs," she objected. "I didn't even know he had them. I'm completely innocent. If I get 25 years in prison, my baby will be grown and married when I get out. I'll miss all of her childhood. This just can't be happening to me. I'm innocent. Whatever happened to 'innocent until proven guilty'?" she asked the public defender that was assigned to her case.

"Oh, the state plans to prove you're guilty, all right. They found the drugs in your bag, and Greg is going to be their star witness." Laura stood and turned to walk away.

"But ..." the public defender continued, then hesitated.

Laura stopped, turned around, and sat back down. She realized that he may have something to say that could offer her hope. At this point, she certainly didn't have any.

"Just so you know, the prosecutor has already agreed to reduce the charges to possession rather than trafficking, if we can work out a plea. Of course, the judge will have to agree to the terms, but the penalty for possession is two to five years, and the judge has broad discretion. He can even grant probation, if he so chooses."

Laura went limp with relief.

"But we will be prepared to go to trial if we can't work out a plea. The choice will be yours, but you will have all the information you need to help you make that choice. There are two other attorneys with an interest in the case, so you will have the best defense possible."

She wanted to crawl through the window and kiss the man. She was so grateful, she was unable to speak. Tears were rolling down her face as she stood and placed both hands on her chest. She could only hope that he saw the gratitude on her face as she nodded to him, mouthed "thank you," and headed back to her cell. She couldn't wait to call her mom and give her the good news. She never thought she would see the day when two to five years in prison would seem like such a good deal. She realized that she had made a stupid decision to let a stranger carry her bag in the airport when the voice on the loud speaker keep repeating warnings about the very trap that she fell into.

"However this turns out," Laura said out loud, "somehow, I know I can make it from here."

When you're in the airport, don't allow anyone to carry your bags. And don't carry or hold anyone's bag, not even while they go to the restroom. Remember, if you are caught with a bag containing drugs, and the true owner does not claim owner-ship, you are going to jail. It never occurred to Laura that Greg would place drugs in her baby's bag. But she didn't know anything about Greg, and she made

MORAL LESSON

a mistake that could cause her to serve time in prison because she trusted her bag to a stranger who *seemed* like a nice person.

CHAPTER

3

USING THE
WRONG NAME

Clara Hunter King

elvin, a handsome 22 year old who couldn't keep a job, sang along with the rapper as he cruised down Spring Street in Winston, Georgia. He was driving his girlfriend's convertible PT Cruiser. He saw the light ahead change to yellow and decided to speed up to make the light. He was not in any particular hurry, but just didn't want to wait through the light. He uttered a curse word when he saw the blue flashing light in the rearview mirror. He pulled over and stopped the car. He started to make a run for it when he remembered that he had an outstanding traffic ticket, but he decided to stay put and not make any movement when he saw the officer approaching with his hand on his weapon. He placed both hands on the steering wheel.

"Roll down the window," the officer said. Melvin kept his right hand on the steering wheel and rolled down the window with his left hand.

"Let me see your driver's license and proof of insurance."

"Okay," Melvin said. "They are in my wallet, which is in the glove compartment." Placing his left hand on the steering wheel, he opened the glove compartment with his right hand, then used both hands to flip through the wallet. He pulled out the insurance card and handed it to the officer. Then he continued to search for his driver's license that he knew he didn't have with him.

"I know I have my license, officer, give me just a minute."

"Just step out of the car," the officer said.

Melvin stepped out of the car and went through each pocket in his pants and jacket. He looked through the wallet again and kept patting his sides.

"That's okay," said the officer. "Just move around to the back of the vehicle; I'll check it out. What's your name?"

"Michael ... Michael Davis," Melvin said. The officer moved over to the patrol car and called headquarters to check for a driver's license for Michael Davis. Melvin began to regret choosing such a common name. He wished he had chosen a more unique name. Melvin grew nervous because it was taking the officer so long. He squirmed around and cursed himself for not paying the ticket he had gotten almost a year earlier. After what seemed like a very long time to Melvin, the officer moved over to him as he placed his hand on his weapon.

"Turn around and put your hands on the vehicle."

"What seems to be the problem?" Melvin asked, as he turned and placed his hands on the vehicle. The officer patted Melvin down, then reached for his handcuffs.

"You are under arrest for auto theft. You have the right to remain silent. Anything you say can and will be used against you in a court of law. You have the right to have an attorney represent you. If you can't afford one, one will be appointed for you.

"Now put your hands behind your back."

"I didn't steal no car," Melvin protested as he placed his hands behind his back. "All I did wrong was get a ticket and not pay it. My name is Melvin Manning."

"Yeah, right," the officer said as he snapped the handcuffs on Melvin.

"I swear—you can call my mom. Let me use my cell phone. You can ask her. She can describe me." Melvin felt sick because he couldn't convince the officer to check his story out. He tried to convince the officer to run a check on Melvin Manning and verify his identity.

"If you look up my correct name, you will see that I'm not Michael Davis. You can tell who I am by my name, my height, weight, and address. When you pull up my name, I'll tell you my address and you can see that it's me. Otherwise, how would I know the address? That's a way to prove that I'm who I say I am."

The officer was not interested in what Melvin had to say. He called for a wrecker to tow Melvin's girlfriend's car and ushered Melvin to the patrol car.

As Melvin walked to the car, tears ran down his face. He was sure the officer could verify his identity if he took the time to check. Melvin begged the officer to check out his correct name.

"If I check Melvin Manning and find that he has a warrant for his arrest, what name will you use then? If you lied once, why should I believe you are telling the truth now?" the officer asked sarcastically.

"I swear," Melvin said.

"Yeah, right, tell it to the judge," the officer said as he opened the back door and motioned for Melvin to get in. As Melvin walked past the officer, he turned and kicked him on the leg. The officer stumbled and fell forward to the ground. Melvin ran. The officer gave chase and caught Melvin as he tried to climb over a fence. He struck Melvin in the side with his nightstick. Melvin was sure he heard his ribs crack. He screamed and fell to the ground. The officer stomped him in the back, then Melvin turned onto his side and rolled up in a fetal position. The officer kicked Melvin's rear end and cursed him. Melvin could only groan and rock.

"Get up, you idiot," the officer yelled.

"My ribs are broken. I can't breath." Melvin began to gasp for breath as the officer yanked him to his feet. He went limp and fell back to the ground. The officer cursed him and called for an ambulance. Melvin lay on the ground and pretended to be unconscious. *If he thinks I'm okay, he'll probably kill be before the ambulance arrives, and it's all Michael Davis's fault. Why did the idiot have to go and steal a car?*

When the ambulance arrived, Melvin was groaning but would not open his eyes. He appeared to be having trouble breathing. The officer explained that he had to strike him with the nightstick in self-defense. He lifted his pants and showed the emergency crew the red mark on his leg. One of the technicians lifted Melvin's shirt and touched his rib cage. It was already beginning to swell. Melvin jerked and groaned.

"Can you speak? What's wrong?" the paramedic asked. Melvin merely groaned louder.

"He may very well have a broken rib or two. Let's get him to the hospital," the other paramedic said.

Melvin was still in handcuffs as they loaded him on a stretcher and pushed him into the ambulance. The tow truck arrived as the ambulance pulled away from the curb. Melvin could hear the motor and knew it was the tow truck coming to take his girlfriend's car away.

Melvin was checked into the hospital as Michael Davis, and no one paid any attention to him when he tried to tell them that he was Melvin Manning. He asked the nurse to call his mom. The message on the answering machine said she was attending a family reunion in Las Vegas and would not be back in until Friday. Melvin did not have access to a phone and was placed in a room with a deputy stationed outside his door.

"Can't you call her?" Melvin asked when the nurse told him about the message. "They are staying at the Mirage Hotel in Las Vegas."

"It wouldn't do any good. We can't change your name without some form of identification. Does anyone else live with you and your mother?"

"Yes, my twin brother, Kelvin, but he never answers my mother's phone or listens to her messages. We both have our own cell phone, but I can't remember his number. Can't someone go to my house and get my brother?"

"I'm sorry, Mr. Davis, but we can't help you with that," the nurse said. Melvin had never been so frustrated. His mom had begged him to go to the family reunion with her. Each year he promised her he would, and at the last minute, he always found an excuse not to go. He knew his mom left for Las Vegas that morning, and he had not even bothered to go home to say goodbye.

Melvin was in the hospital for two days. It turned out that he did have three broken ribs, and he had a sore behind where the officer kicked him. But he was going to be okay. His mom came home two days after he was released from the hospital and taken to the county jail. Melvin had called home to try and leave a message, but there was no one to accept the call. He had a long time to think about his relationship with his mom and his brother. His brother had not even missed him or been concerned about him.

They didn't see each other or talk to each other very often. He could probably count the times on one hand that he had called his brother on his cell phone.

Kelvin was always working; Melvin was never able to keep a job for more than a week. His mom paid his cell phone bill, and his girlfriend let him drive her car. He would drop her off at work and keep her car. Sometimes he didn't even pick her up on time. He realized what a jerk he was as he sat in the cell and thought about his life. He called his girlfriend to let her know how sorry he was about her car. She thanked him and asked him to erase her phone number from his mind and his phone book, then hung up on him.

"It's their fault," he said out loud. "Why do women allow men to get away with such foolishness?" He was disgusted with himself, with his mom, and with his girlfriend.

He vowed that he would change. He would develop a relationship with his brother and keep his next job. He would show the proper respect for his mom and his girlfriend—if she ever agreed to take him back.

Melvin waited to be sure his mom was home before he called her. She answered on the first ring. She knew he had not been home because there were no dirty dishes in the sink, but it seemed that someone else had been there. After he explained how he had ended up in jail and she had agreed to put her house up for the $20,000 bail, she informed

41

him that this was the last time she would put her house up to get him out of jail. He promised that he would never end up in jail again. Then she asked Melvin about the missing items from the house.

"You wouldn't, by any chance, have moved my microwave oven and small electric can opener that Kelvin bought me for Christmas, would you?"

"No," Melvin said. "Is anything else missing?"

"I don't think so."

"Go look in my room and see if all three of my coats are all the way to the wall on the right-hand side of my closet. They are all together. Mama, if you hurry, I may be able to hang on while you check. My time is almost up." Melvin's mind was racing. He was trying to figure out who would have broken into their house. He knew that no one would break into a house just to take a microwave oven and electric can opener.

Melvin's friend, BJ, took the microwave and can opener as an afterthought. He and his buddy had gone to the house to steal some name-brand clothes from Melvin and his brother. BJ had called Melvin's mom, as he often did when he couldn't reach Melvin on his cell phone. He would ask her to tell Melvin to turn his phone on. When he got the recording stating that she was in Las Vegas and wouldn't be back until Friday, he immediately called his buddy, Fried Chicken.

"Let's go shopping at The Boz Store."

"Man, have you lost your mind. Where are we going to get money to go shopping at The Boz Store?" Fried Chicken asked.

"We don't need any money. The clothes are already in someone's home just waiting for us to take them. The homeowner won't be back home until Friday. Her two sons won't be home. One works all the time, and the other one hangs out with his girl most of the time. With the mom out of town, he will be hanging out with his girl so she can feed him. So, while he's lying around freeloading off his girl, we'll just load some of those name-brand clothes into our car, and no one will ever know who did it."

"And just how do we get in?"

"They keep a key in a magnetic box under the dryer vent behind the house."

"How do you know that?" Fried Chicken asked.

"One night we took Melvin home and he asked us to pull the car in back of the house and shine the lights on the vent so he could locate the box with the key."

Fried Chicken and BJ retrieved the key and went in to take some of the name-brand clothes Melvin and Kelvin owned.

"Let's just take about half," BJ said. "No need in being greedy; after all, Melvin is my friend."

When Melvin's mom looked in his closet, she discovered that his three coats were gone. She could see that a lot of his other clothes were missing also. She went into Kelvin's room and discovered that some of his clothes were missing.

"Kids!" she said in disgust out loud. "Probably some of Melvin's friends." She rushed back to the phone and told Melvin what she had found. He felt sick and angry and tired. The guard held up one finger to let him know his time was about over. He knew he was going to have a bad night.

When Melvin's mom attempted to use her house to post his bail, she discovered that she would need Kelvin's signature. She had added his name to her deed because she knew he was more responsible than Melvin and she wanted him to be in charge in case something happened to her. After talking with the attorney who checked out all the details, she discovered some hard cold facts that she had not realized. She sat down and made a list of what she learned the hard way.

Lessons Learned the Hard Way

1. When you add someone's name to your deed as joint tenant with right of survivorship, you are giving that person a fifty percent interest in your home.

2. Her intent to just make sure Kelvin was in charge in case something happened to her had not been accomplished. If she died, the house would belong to Kelvin outright, and Melvin would have no share in it.

3. If you add someone's name to your deed and that person acquires debts, or already has outstanding debts, such as back taxes, child support, or a monetary judgment against them, a lien can be placed on your house, and the lien must be paid before you can use any equity in your home for any reason, even to refinance your home.

4. The IRS had placed a lien for $30,000 on her house for back taxes Kelvin owed. Kelvin had never filed a tax return during his three years of operating a business. Although he had large contracts, he used most of the money to pay his contractors and buy tools and supplies.

5. Even though Kelvin agreed to sign his interest in the house back over to her, he was unable to do so because the back taxes to the IRS would have to be paid before they would remove the lien.

45

6. And finally, if you don't know what you are doing, ask some knowledgeable person. Don't take advice about how to handle your property from a friend who doesn't even own a bicycle.

Mom was disgusted that she had added Kelvin to her deed based on the advice of a friend who didn't know anything about real property issues. Kelvin was disgusted because he had received the letters from IRS, asking him to file his tax returns. He thought that nothing would happen if he just ignored them. He didn't want to bother with all that paperwork. Melvin was the most disgusted of all because he had to remain in jail.

A public defender finally presented evidence to the court to prove that Melvin was not Michael Davis and convinced the officer and prosecutor to dismiss the battery charge against Melvin. After all, Melvin had suffered three broken ribs and a lump on his backside at the hands of the officer. The auto theft charge against him was dismissed after three months in jail.

Melvin was surprised to see both his mom and brother when he was brought into the courtroom. His brother had not been back to court with him since his first court appearance over four years earlier. Now they were trying to readjust their lives and become a close family. Melvin thought he was going home. But to his surprise, there was a hold on him for the traffic ticket warrant. He had to serve a mandatory ten days on that warrant. He was permitted to visit with his family before returning to jail. After they had all had a good cry and hugged each other, Kelvin did what he had decided to do more often in the future. He gave his brother some advice.

"Be thankful it's just ten days for a traffic ticket. That's a lot better than ten years for car theft." They laughed and hugged each other again. At that moment, they all felt that the healing process for their family had begun. Melvin was taken away to serve his ten days and Mom and Kelvin went home to wait for his release, with the hope that they would all experience a new lease on life.

MORAL LESSON

Melvin's troubles began with a speeding ticket, but he could have easily taken care of that by paying the ticket. He learned the hard way that ignoring problems do not make them go away.

That mistake cost him three months jail time, money for attorney fees that his family could not afford, and a felony arrest on his record. Even though the charge was dismissed, the felony arrest will not automatically be removed from his record. Remember, if you use someone else's name, they may be in more trouble than you, and the judicial system does not have any obligation to prove your identity.

Melvin's brother learned a valuable lesson about taxes. If the IRS has a record of your income and you don't file your tax return, they will file it for you. And they do not have any obligation to try and figure out if you have any deductions or paid others part of the money. You will be taxed on the entire amount. So, ignoring problems do not make them go away, but it may cause you to *go*—to jail or in debt to the IRS.

CHAPTER

4

The Excitment
is Gone
Bob's Story

Yvonne Hawks

thought that I was seeing things. "Was that Bill?" I said to myself. *Come on and get a grip, Bob.* I knew that could not have been Bill because the boy was just about the same age that Bill was when I last saw him. After we left Bill in the car that night, I saw him once in the hospital.

Bill asked me if I knew Johnny's real name, and, of course, I had to say no. Johnny never came back to school after that night, and I never looked for him.

At the hospital we sat there in almost dead silence until Bill said, "Don't worry, Bob, I won't give you up now. What point would there be?"

I couldn't say a word. My mouth was dry, and I couldn't even swallow. I guess I was relieved that he would keep quiet about me because I knew that they would arrest me, too. Yeah, I didn't know what to say when I saw Bill handcuffed to the bed with a guard outside of his door. I had to tell the guard that I was his brother and our mom was sick and couldn't come to see him. So I had to lie to get in to see him.

That was the longest ten minutes of my life. We didn't talk about much of anything, especially not that night. When the time was up, I just walked away and never looked back. Not a day goes by that I don't think about Bill and that night. I should have said something, but I was too scared and too ashamed.

After we bailed out of the car, I was hiding in the bushes and could see Bill on the ground.

I saw his feet, his legs, and then the faces of people as someone rolled him over. I didn't move or say a word. One of the officers pulled Bill up by his shirt. They kept asking him who the others were, but he never said a word. They kept shaking him and yelling, "Who are they? Where do they live?" Bill never knew what was going on. He didn't even know that the car was stolen. This never should have happened to him.

I tried to move to help, but I couldn't. I even thought that if I came out, maybe they would stop shaking Bill, but I didn't want to go to jail. I knew that I was going to jail if they saw me. So I just kept hiding, and I have been hiding ever since.

Earlier that evening, Johnny and I were hanging out at the mall, waiting for Bill to get off work. Before going to Burger Hut, we were walking around, checking out the people. Johnny spotted a lady going to her car with a lot of packages.

"Hey, Bob. Do you see what I see?" he asked.

I looked straight ahead and saw the lady juggling her packages. Johnny once told me that he would boost cars at the mall from people who carried a lot of packages. He said that it's easy to take their car because they are so preoccupied with other things.

We followed the lady outside to her car. She was just juggling, trying to get to her car. Once she got there, she opened her door and put her purse inside. We were ready to make our move, but someone suddenly came up behind us.

"Man, we almost had it," Johnny complained.

"Why don't we just go by and hook up with Bill?" I asked. I didn't want Johnny to know that I really didn't want to steal a car because knowing Johnny, he would get bent out of shape and take it out on me. He wasn't listening to a word I had to say. We just keep walking around the parking lot, trying to jack a car. Finally, Johnny saw one and took it. The doors were left unlocked, but Johnny had to bust the steering column. It didn't take him long at all. If I didn't know better, I would have thought that Johnny had a key. We pulled out of the parking lot and headed over to pick up Bill. The Burger Hut was not that far away. It was almost time for Billy to leave work.

We walked into Burger Hut and ordered a couple of sodas. Bill wouldn't give us the hookup even though Johnny would ask every time. If Jason were there, he would throw in an order of fries or give it to us half price or something like that. Jason is another friend of ours, but he doesn't work at

53

Burger Hut anymore. He said that he got tired of the manager always complaining about his cash drawer being short of money or the money not adding up to the amount of food that was sold.

Johnny always said, "What difference would it make, Bill? Burger Hut makes a lot of money and won't miss a couple of drinks or fries. Besides, you can tell them that you drank them or ate the food. You know that you can give your family discounts."

"Yeah, Johnny, I can give family discounts and can eat anything while I'm at work, but who's going to believe that I ate all of those fries and drank all of those sodas? Like they would believe that! I can't give you free food every time you come in. They'll fire me. Besides, they know my family, and you don't look anything like them."

Bill would laugh it off but would look very uncomfortable. I could feel the pressure that Johnny was putting on him. If I had only stood up to Johnny about taking the car, then Bill wouldn't have gotten hurt. I was just going along with Johnny, hoping that he wouldn't find a car and then maybe he would give up, but that didn't happen. We found that car, and now we are at Burger Hut, waiting for Bill. The best thing that could happen now is that Johnny would forget about the car and we leave it in the parking lot.

Bill had clocked out and was ready to go. We went outside and started walking to the car. I remember thinking to myself, *Why doesn't Bill ask about the car, and then we both could try to talk Johnny out of driving it?* We got closer and closer to the car, just talking and shooting the breeze. Bill paused for a moment and looked kind of funny, but he climbed into the backseat of it. Johnny drove off, and everything else is history.

The police never found me in the bushes, and I never came forward to help Bill. Without bringing attention to myself, I learned that Bill was hurt really badly, but no one could give me the details. When I saw Bill in the hospital, the only thing that I could think of is whether or not he was going to tell the police about me. Selfish, I know. You could only imagine the relief I felt when he said that he wasn't going to tell them about me.

Now I work at the courthouse as a deputy. Ironic, isn't it. The job isn't bad, but if someone had told me while I was in high school that I would be working in law enforcement after graduation, I would have laughed at them. I had worked the streets for about two and a half years before I was assigned to the courthouse.

You see a lot of things working in the courthouse, but I never thought that I would see Bill. I took a closer look at the young boy walking down the hall towards me. It wasn't Bill, but he was a real good look-alike. He was acting like almost every other young fellow that comes through these halls. They act so tough and appear to know everything, even if they are scared out of their wits. Some of them have their mothers and fathers with them, and then others have only their mothers. Few come with their fathers. This boy was lucky—he had both parents. Then I saw who was behind him—it was Bill. He was behind the boy in a wheelchair, accompanied by a pretty lady.

Should I let him know that I am here, or should I just hide again? I have experience in hiding. I'll talk to Bill.

"Hello, Bill."

Bill looked up at me and didn't say anything at first. I thought that maybe he didn't recognize me. It has been a long time since we saw each other and things change, people change. He rolled up closer without saying anything. Finally he spoke.

"Is that you, Bob?"

"Yeah, I thought that I was seeing things when I saw you." I pointed at his son as the boy stood there with his hands in his pockets, trying to ignore the fact that I was there.

"He takes after his mother with his looks. Barbara, this is Bob."

"Hello," Barbara said. "Good to meet you. You know Bill?"

"Yeah, we went to high school together."

"You did? Bill doesn't talk much about his high school days. Did you know him well?"

"Barbara, catch up with Jerrod," Bill said sharply. Barbara looked a little bewildered, but she walked on.

"It was good to meet you, Bob," she said as she walked away.

"You too, Barbara. Bill, it's been a long time. I've thought about you on and off."

"You have? I really haven't had time to think about much of anything. My family and my son, they need me."

"What's going on? Maybe I can help," Bob said.

"No," he said sharply as he rolled away.

Bill had never been much of a talker, but I guess that it wasn't quite right to ask him to open up to me. Needless to say, I was like a stranger to him. It's been a while since we've seen each other and the last time we were together, I let him down. How could he trust me now when he couldn't trust me before?

The day went on and eventually Bill and his family came back out of the courtroom. He almost rolled right by me, and then he spun around.

"Hey, man, I'm sorry about how I acted earlier. I just had so much on my mind."

"That's OK. I understand," I said. I wasn't sure what to think or what to say. He had every right not to ever speak to me again, but I was so glad that he stopped.

"When do you get off?" asked Bill.

"Five o'clock."

"Do you want to get a beer?"

"That sounds great." I finally exhaled. The situation was so tense and uncomfortable. I was so grateful that he asked me to get a drink with him.

"Do you know where Choco's is, on 47th Street?"

"Yeah."

57 ⚖

"See you around 6:30 p.m.?" Bill asked.

"Sounds good."

Maybe this could be the start to mending our friendship. One can only hope. I looked forward to seeing Bill tonight. I hoped that I could stand up and be brave and not be afraid this time.

CHAPTER

5

Jessica's home for the Summer

Yvonne Hawks

essica was home for the summer and working at the local department store during the day. It was not hard work, but she was a bit nervous at the beginning. She had never worked a cash register and didn't want to mess up. Jessica wanted to talk with her mother about the job but didn't want her mom to know just how nervous she was. After about two weeks, the store was going to put Jessica on the cash register alone.

"Mom, they're going to let me run a register by myself tomorrow," Jessica said.

"That's good, Jessica. Do you feel comfortable with that?"

"Yeah, I guess so. I've been running the register myself for a while now. Tara has just been looking over my shoulder for about a week. You remember, Tara is the one who trained me."

Tara had been at the store for about 25 years. She began working there right after graduating from high school. She was nice enough, but she didn't seem to be happy with her job. It was the little things that she said and how she acted that made Jessica think she wasn't happy. Tara would come into work right at the time she was to be on the floor. She wasn't late, but she was never early. Tara would comment that she was scheduled to work from 8 a.m. to 4:30 p.m. and not a minute longer. She would also say something smart like, "They don't pay me enough to do that," or "I get paid by the hour and not by the job."

Jessica went to work every day and was always on time. She had not gone out all summer. Then one night, she said to her mother, "I'm going to Club-T with Jackie."

"Who's driving?" asked her mom.

"I am. I'll pick her up at her house."

"OK, just be careful."

"I always am," Jessica said before she went out the door.

Jessica's mom knew and liked Jackie. She was a sweet girl, and her mom felt that Jessica would drive safely, despite the two tickets she had gotten before she went off to school.

Jessica arrived at Jackie's house, then off they went.

"Stop by the school first," Jackie said.

"Why?"

"To get Karen."

"Oh, I didn't know that Karen was going."

"Yeah, you know Karen, don't you? She was in our English class, and she said that she would drive."

"Yeah, I know Karen." Jessica didn't think much about it. She drove straight to the school where Karen was waiting.

Karen was a bold, aggressive person, and she had been in a little trouble with the law. Some girls started a fight with her, and she cut them up. Not just one, but *all* of them. It wasn't a little scratch because one of the girls needed 52 stitches. It's not clear how long the other girls were in the hospital, but they were out of school for a long time and Karen went to jail. Then she had to report to her probation officer all last year. She also had to do some kind of community service and could not have any contact with the girls. So if the four girls were in the lunchroom, Karen couldn't be in there. But all in all, Karen was a nice person. She was probably a good person to have on your side, if you were in a fight.

When they arrived at the high school, Karen was waiting with Temiko. Neither Jessica nor Jackie knew Temiko. They got right out of Jessica's car and into Karen's car. Their night had begun.

At the club, they were having a good time. The band was good, and the crowd was jumping. Karen was able to get a drink from somewhere. She was only 18 years old and knew that she was not old enough to drink, and the bartender should have known better. Jessica took a taste of Karen's drink.

63

Karen supplied them all with a taste of her drinks. When they left the club, Karen was driving. This time, Jessica was in the front seat. Karen had brought her cup out to the car.

The club smelled like old beer and cigarettes, and so did the girls. On the way home, Karen stopped at a restaurant to use the bathroom. When she drove off, she forgot to turn on her lights. Almost immediately, the police pulled up behind them. Karen didn't even notice them, and neither did the other three. The police followed them for a short distance and then turned on their blue lights. Karen pulled over in the first lighted parking lot she saw, and the police pulled in right behind her.

When the officer walked up to the car, Karen rolled the window down.

"Miss, did you know that you did not turn on your headlights?"

"No, sir, I'm sorry. The streets lights were so bright, I couldn't tell the difference."

The officer was standing there shining the light into the car when he noticed the cup in the front console.

"Miss, have you been drinking tonight?"

"I had a soda at Club T down the street."

"Is that all?"

"Yes, sir, that's all."

They all knew that was a lie, but they sat there quietly while the officer questioned Karen. Then he asked her to get out of the car and walk back to his car. They couldn't believe it. They all knew that

Karen had more then just a soda that night, and she certainly had more than one drink, even if they didn't know how many. Still, they were willing to let her drive them home.

Jessica and the others tried to see what was going on but couldn't. All of a sudden, a light shone through Jessica's window. They all jumped. There was another officer. He wanted Jessica to roll her window down.

"Ladies, have any of you been drinking?"

Karen and Jessica both said no, but Temiko said yes. But what difference would it make to her because she wasn't driving and she was over 21 years of age. Jackie, Karen, and Jessica were all underage.

"What's in that cup?" the officer asked.

Jessica looked at the cup and then up at the officer. "I don't know," she said.

"What do you mean you don't know? It's yours, isn't it?"

"No."

"No, what?"

"It's not mine."

"What's not yours?"

"That drink."

"So, it's a drink?"

"No!"

"Now it's not a drink. I thought that you said that you didn't know what it was."

"I don't. You got that light in my face, and I got confused."

"Have you been drinking?"

"No!"

"Just tell me the truth; it'll go easier on you if you do."

"No, not really."

"Not really? So you *have* been drinking."

"No, I just had a sip."

"OK, you all. Get out of the car. Show me some ID."

They all piled out, nervous and scared. The officer took their licenses and went back to his car. By then, they had put Karen into the police car. The officers searched the car. They smelled the liquid in the cup and poured it out. After they finished searching the car, the officers gave Jessica and Jackie a ticket for underage drinking. Karen was taken to jail, and Temiko was not allowed to drive the car because she had admitted to drinking. But Temiko was the only one who did not receive a ticket because she was not driving and she was over 21 years old.

MORAL LESSON

Had Jessica just stayed in her own car and drove, as she led her mother to believe, this may not have happened. No matter how tempting it way be, if you are not 21 years old, you can not drink. A sip is still a drink. Always exercise your right to remain silent. Jessica was saying things that she really didn't mean. Finally, don't get into a car with a person who has been drinking even if you believe they are not drunk. Karen's mistake of not turning on her headlights was the start of everything.

CHAPTER

6

Two Tickets—

You're Out!

Yvonne Hawks

essica was such a good kid. She was on the honor roll, she worked in her church, and she was liked by all who knew her. Now she's 17 years old and has her driver's license. She complained about how hard it was to get her driver's license. Although she was very responsible for a teenager, she was still a teenager facing decisions that she had never faced before. One day she called her mother at work with a surprise, but somehow, her mother was not surprised.

"Mom, this is Jessica," she said.

"Hi, sweetie. Where are you?" said Mom.

"I'm on Green Street. I hit this lady from the rear." Then came the longest pause Jessica had ever experienced with her mother.

"Well, Jessica, are you alright?" her mom asked.

"Yeah." Jessica sounded as if she was about to cry. Her heart was in her throat, and she was feeling sick to her stomach. She explained to her mother what had occurred. The accident happened because the other driver decided to turn right instead of going straight through the intersection at the last moment.

"Do you need me to come pick you up?" Jessica's mom asked.

"No. I'm alright. I just wanted to tell you that the officer wrote me a ticket. He said that there was no damage, but since he was called, he had to write me a ticket. I don't understand why he couldn't just let me go. The other person said that it was alright with her."

The officer knew from experience that people say that it's alright at the moment, but later, they find damages and have no record of the incident.

"OK, Jessica, then go straight home," her mom said. "Just be careful on your way, and I'll see you there when I get off work."

At this point, Jessica couldn't tell whether her mom was surprised or mad with her. The two of them were very close. They talked about almost everything, and they went almost everywhere together. It was hard to imagine one without the other. They had a very trusting relationship. Jessica was very mature for her age and hung around her mom as much as possible. She had always been so careful and responsible. At least she had been in front of her mom. But her mom wasn't giving Jessica's driving the close attention she gave other aspects of Jessica's life.

Jessica had great reflexes because she played basketball, tennis, and every other sport you can name. And she drove like she played sports. She was very aggressive, and she drove to win. The tighter the traffic, the better she liked it. She viewed traffic like players on the court, and it was her goal to get through the hole, make that shot, and score.

After Jessica's mom got home that day, they talked about what had happened again and how Jessica could have avoided the accident. Her mom was not mad with her but wanted Jessica to make this a learning experience and to be more careful in the future. She knew that accidents can happen no matter what you do or how careful you were.

Her mom was also concerned about how this could affect Jessica's confidence and desire to drive. She remembered a friend that she had a long time ago when it wasn't as hard to get a driver's license. You could just go to the license office and ask for your learner's license and a driver's handbook as long as you had one of your parents with you, and your parents didn't even have to have a driver's license. Then to get your permanent real driver's license, an adult could take you to take the written test and drive around the parking lot. There you have it—your very own license.

Jessica's mom said her friend had just started driving when she hit a little boy. The child had simply run out into the street. The little boy was hurt, but he recovered. Mom's friend was never the same. She stopped driving for years. She was 16 years old when it happened, and she was about 31 years old before she drove again.

When the officer gave Jessica the ticket, he told her how she could call in and find out how much her ticket would be and where to go to pay it instead of going to court. Jessica and her mom went in to pay her ticket one afternoon. It took every bit of ten minutes. They went shopping after that since her Mom had taken off for the rest of the day. Jessica wasn't in the mood to shop because her mom made her pay the ticket. It cost Jessica $150.

As the year went on, Jessica was enjoying herself in her senior year of high school. Just like every red-blooded American teenager, she was having the time of her life living for the moment, but the moment got interrupted again. She saw the blue lights in her rearview mirror and felt the same feeling she experienced when she hit the lady several months earlier. Jessica's love for speeding down the road had caused her to get another ticket. This was her second ticket in less than a year. She told her mother about this ticket too. They agreed to call about the fine again. To their surprise, Jessica had to pay $287. It was a good thing that Jessica was working part-time because her mom just did not have any extra money to pay the ticket. But it still hurt because Jessica was working to save for her college tuition.

Jessica finally graduated with honors and left for college. She was so excited to be going but nervous to be away from home. She knew that this was only the beginning of her adulthood. She met a lot of new people and made new friends. Only a few of the students in her dorm had cars. Jessica had her opportunity to drive, nevertheless. One of her friends had a car and sometimes Jessica would drive when they went places. Jessica could remember having to parallel park for Pat one day. The cars were very tight, but this was the closest spot to their dorm. Jessica got into the driver's seat and put that car into that space without a hitch.

When Jessica came home for spring break, she had to renew her driver's license and so did her mother. They both went together. As her mother waited in line, Jessica came up to her with a bewildered look on her face.

"What's going on, Jessica?" her mom asked.

"My license is suspended," she said in disbelief. They just couldn't understand it. After her mom finished getting her license renewed, they went to inquire about Jessica's license. They were told that her license had been suspended for over a year. This was shortly after her second ticket. They still could not understand why it was suspended and why she had not been notified. The clerk explained to them that the two tickets Jessica had gotten in a 12-month period put her over the maximum number of points allowed by law for a driver her age. Her license had automatically been suspended when she received the second ticket. Also, they said that the notice of this suspension was sent by mail to the address listed on her driver's license. After looking closer at the record, the clerk couldn't find where they had notified Jessica about her license suspension. Jessica's mom said that as she was Jessica's mother, she should have been notified of the suspension. The clerk explained that only the driver would be notified of the suspension even though Jessica was a minor. To get Jessica's license reinstated, she had to take a defensive driving course and pay a reinstatement fee to the Department of Motor Vehicles.

Jessica couldn't believe that she had been driving for over a year with a suspended driver's license. Each day last summer, Jessica would drive about 40 miles one way to go to work. Not only that, she would run errands for her mother, go places by herself, and she was driving other people's cars at school. She was horrified by the thought of what would have happened if she had been arrested for driving on a suspended license out of state. After they left the driver's license bureau, Jessica's mom decided to contact an attorney.

"This is not right, Jessica," she said. "No one notified us that your license was suspended. Now you must pay for a driving course and pay $210 to have your license reinstated. You have already paid $150 for the first ticket and $287 for the speeding ticket. That's just not fair. We're going to talk with an attorney and get this taken care of."

Jessica's mom was fortunate to work for an employer who had legal insurance. She was able to get a free consultation. She explained to the attorney the situation and wanted to know how she could get Jessica's license reinstated without Jessica having to take the driving course and pay the reinstatement fee. She thought that since Department of Motor Vehicles dropped the ball about notifying Jessica about her suspension, they should just call it even and give Jessica her license back. The attorney was very sympathetic, but there was nothing that he could do for her now.

"I don't understand," she said. "They never notified Jessica about the suspension. Can't they just take it back?"

"The law is clear. Jessica's tickets suspended her license, and the only way that she can get her license back is to take that driving course and pay the money. You came to me too late."

"Too late! What do you mean?"

"Notice of the suspension does not stop the license from being suspended. No notice only helps if she was stopped for driving on a suspended license. She must know that her license was suspended at the time she is driving to be convicted of driving on a suspended license."

"Oh, I didn't know that."

"You should have called me before she paid the tickets."

"Why?"

"Some jurisdictions have programs for youthful offenders that your daughter may have been able to take advantage of. That may have stopped her license from being suspended. You need to consider this with other types of charges. But my first advice is to consult an attorney if you are not sure."

"I didn't know that."

"There is no guarantee, but it would have been worth taking a look at it. Since you had legal insurance, it wouldn't have cost you anything but a little time. Also, Jessica could have gone to court to see if there was some sort of alternative action she could have done."

"Go to court?" Jessica exclaimed.

"Yes, go to court. Just paying the ticket means that you are saying that you're guilty. There were a lot of things that you could have done to help with these tickets besides just paying them. It's good that you wanted to take responsibility for your actions, but you must be smart about what you do and know how it will affect you."

Well, Jessica and her mom left the attorney's office very dissatisfied, but better informed. They hope that they will never be in this situation again, but if they are, they will most likely make different decisions.

Jessica enrolled in her class and her mom drove her every night. On the first night after class, several people got into their cars and drove away. These were all people with suspended licenses who were not suppose to drive. Jessica was surprised and bewildered. When she told her mom, her mother assured Jessica that she would not be driving until she got her license reinstated. She reminded Jessica what the attorney had said: "The penalty for driving on a suspended license is much more severe than the fines you just paid—you go to jail."

Jessica agreed that not driving was a wise decision. She completed her class and paid her fees. Altogether, those two tickets cost Jessica and her family about $887, a lot of time, and quite a bit of inconvenience.

Jessica thought she did everything right, she told her mom about the two tickets, she paid the fines, finished the defensive driving class, and took responsibility for her actions. Even doing the right thing can be tricky and expensive, but when you keep disobeying the law just because you can pay the fine, you need to know that you are *not* doing the right thing.

MORAL LESSON

Taking responsibility for your actions is admiral. But you need to be aware of the law and how it can affect you in order to make an informed decision. The law may vary from jurisdiction to jurisdiction. Parents are a great resource of information and guidance in situations like this. Sometimes even they may need to ask someone else for help. It is recommended to consult with an attorney on legal matters. It may save you time, money and in a case like this, possibly your license.

CHAPTER

7

One Dance

Too Many

Janine Brooks-Collier

"I see you looking at me, and you know I want to love you, winding and grinding up on the floor," was blaring in Nicky's basement. My outfit was on point, and my hair was bouncing and flowing, and JT was giving me the look. I knew he was Shameka's man, but he was a cutie, and he was rocking all the latest gear. JT approached and asked me to dance. I couldn't say no. All eyes were on us. He was singing the song to me, and I was singing it back, and I was winding, and he was grinding.

JT and I danced one song after another. I have to admit I really liked his flow. JT was the quarterback of the football team. Everyone loves JT, from the teachers to all the other kids. All the guys thought he was cool, and all the girls wanted to be his main lady. As I left the party and JT walked me to the top of the stairs, I noticed Shameka's girls all huddled up, whispering, pointing, and snickering. I was wondering what all the hard stares were for. All night they kept looking and rolling their eyes—

even before I started dancing with JT. The girls at my school were always fighting over some boy. I didn't have a boyfriend, and I wasn't looking. Although if I *was* looking, JT would be the boy I would be trying to get with. But there was no sense in me even thinking about JT, or any other boy, for that matter. My parents were strict, and my brothers and sister were snitches. I could never pull it off.

I looked back at the crowd of haters, and I kept it moving. I wish they knew I was only having fun and I loved to dance. Wow! All those looks—it's not like JT and Shameka were married. We were seniors in high school. Besides, I was only daydreaming about JT. I was more interested in college and all the things my parents promised me if I could just continue on the path I was going.

Oh, well, I left just in time to make my curfew, and it was a good thing because my parents were still up watching TV and chitchatting. I went to my room and lay across my bed. I loved my high school. We were the best in football, and my cheerleading squad went all the way to Nationals. I felt like I was on top of the world. I was almost guaranteed a full ride to college, and my dad promised to start letting me drive the family hoopty more often.

It is so funny how things can change overnight and how one bad choice can change your life and your destiny. The hallway was unusually full. I was just walking and feeling happy-go-lucky, humming along with Ciara. All of a sudden, Shameka jumps out with her little cronies, asking why I was all up in her man's face. I just gave her a dirty look and tried to walk past her. Shameka threatened, "Jasmin, stay away from my man!"

I lost it for a minute because I turned and said, "Excuse me, but you might want to talk to your man about that. I am not interested in your man and don't step up to me with all this nonsense."

"Whatever," Shameka replied. She just stood and stared at me for a while. Then she added a few other choice words, smacked her lips, and walked away. Little did I know at lunch it was about to be on. I was surprised by what JT said when he ran up on me.

"Stop running your big mouth to my girl!"

I placed my hands on my hips and begin the "roll your head and point your finger motion," but before I could say anything, JT grabbed me and said, "Do you hear me, girl?"

I jerked my arm away as Shameka appeared suddenly and grabbed my hair and slapped me. Someone from the crowd pulled her away. I turned and kicked JT with everything I had as the teachers and principal approached. JT reached around the teacher and grabbed me by the throat. I tried to reach around the teacher to hit him—anything—to get him to let me go, but I ended up hitting the teacher who ran from the opposite direction.

The next thing I knew, the school police approached and the situation turned very chaotic. The school police were yelling and barking orders and before I could respond, I was shocked with a tazer. I shook uncontrollably, and then lost control of my body functions.

The events moved very rapidly from there. I was suspended from school, my driving privileges were revoked, and I was charged with two counts of affray and terrorist threats. The school resources officer claimed that I threatened JT. *I* was the one who was jumped, JT is twice my size, plus he had help from his stupid girlfriend. My school has a no tolerance fighting rule. To my dismay, I was indicted and charged with a felony, which means I could lose my scholarship. I was really counting on that scholarship to assist me with my college fees. My parents can't afford to send me to college; they barely manage to keep a roof over my head.

My mom fussed and cried more than I have ever seen her fuss and cry before—even more than when my dad comes home a little tipsy. My dad yelled and gave me the beating of my life. I thought about calling DFACS, but I think I deserved that beating.

I think the hurt in my mom's eyes and the disappointment in my father's voice was worse than all the events that led up to my day in court. My parents talked to my grandparents and other family members, and they all got together and hired a great attorney. He was able to get the charges reduced to a misdemeanor, and I received pretrial diversion, and I may still even have a chance at the scholarship. I wish that I hadn't let my mouth and pride run wild. One simple catfight snowballed into a felony charge. My entire family was disappointed in me and couldn't believe I conducted myself in such a manner. My mom was even more disgusted that the whole thing was over a bighead boy. Maybe if I would have just said, "Hey, girl, you know me—I love to dance and that's all it was—just a dance," it would have ended there.

I guess I forget that as students, sometimes our fate is in the hands of the powers that be. We all understand the authorities are not always impartial. I love my school, but they have two sets of rules, and we all know how the man in charge applies those rules.

Most importantly, I was mean to a fellow class-mate just to make myself look better, but in the end, the last laugh was on me. I have since learned to watch my tongue. My mom used to say, "Don't let your mouth overload your butt." Well, my mouth finally overloaded my butt. But the fact that I spent a night in jail and the realization that I could go to prison was enough for me to change my attitude. More importantly, orange, the color of the jail jump-suits, is *not* my color. I also understand that I must always follow the rules in school as well as in society. I saw firsthand how one bad choice can create a huge stumbling block and have negative effects on your life for years to come. Fortunately, I, with the support of my loved ones, am back on the right track and plan to make my parents proud.

CHAPTER
8

Meet Kevin

Betty Williams-Kirby

Kevin was in a good mood when he went to visit his new friend, Stephanie. Her little brother, Brett, a 12 year old, wanted to buy some CDs with the money that he had been saving. Stephanie asked Kevin if he would take them to Peppermint, a store that sells music CDs and videos.

Both Kevin and Stephanie were 17 years old. Kevin had met Stephanie through his friend, Andrew, Stephanie's next-door neighbor. Little did Kevin know that his whole world was about to change.

On that fateful day, Stephanie and Kevin laughed, joked, and sang along with the rappers as they headed towards the music store. Brett sat in the backseat and stared out the window. They made several stops before they reached the music store. The first stop was the Foot Locker. They looked around but didn't buy anything. After a couple of other stops, they finally arrived at the music store. Kevin decided to leave the car door unlocked in case they got separated. That way, the first person to come to the car could get in and wait for the others. When they entered the store, they all wandered off in different directions. Stephanie went to look at some CDs in the rap section, and Kevin stopped up front to fill out a job application. He thought that since he was at the store, he might as well fill out the application. He was, after all, between jobs. Kevin spent about 25 minutes completing the application and talking with the store manager.

When Kevin finished and gave the application to the manager, he went to look for Brett and Stephanie. He located Stephanie first, and they went to find Brett. Stephanie had picked up three CDs she wanted to purchase. She told Kevin about the CDs as they walk around the store, looking for Brett. Finally, they found Brett in the video section.

"Did you find the video you wanted?" Stephanie asked.

"No," Kevin said. "And I don't see anything else I want."

"Okay, I guess we should just head for the cashier," Kevin said.

Kevin walked with Stephanie as she went to pay for her CDs, but he stopped to check out some new CDs on a display rack near the checkout counter. Brett walked ahead of them, left the store, and proceeded out to the car. Kevin didn't find anything he wanted, so he walked through the line, passing Stephanie, and stopped to wait for her near the door. When he looked out the window to see if Brett was in the car, he noticed two men at the car talking with Brett. Kevin had no idea what those two men could be talking to Brett about. He turned and saw that Stephanie was almost finished.

"Hey, Stephanie, I'm going on to the car."

"Okay, I'm right behind you," she replied.

As Kevin walked towards the car, he saw a police car drive up to his car and two officers jumped out of the police car and rushed toward his car. Suddenly, Kevin was filled with a sense of dread. He hesitated for just a moment and turned to see Stephanie walking towards the car. She began to run when she saw the police car and caught up to Kevin.

"What are those police officers doing at your car?" she worriedly asked him.

"I don't know. They just drove up, but the store manager and the other man were already at the car and talking with Brett when I came out of the store."

"What's going on?" Kevin asked as he and Stephanie walked up to the car.

"Seems as if our young friend here helped himself to some merchandise without paying for it," the store manager said.

As Kevin and Stephanie looked into the car, they could see that Brett had removed the backseat of the car and was handing over what seemed to be several CDs and videos. Brett was taking all of this stuff from under the backseat. Kevin and Stephanie were both speechless; neither one of them knew that Brett had stolen this stuff from the store.

The police officers began to ask the store manager and the other man, who turned out to be the theft prevention officer, about the incident.

"Is this the person that came into the store with this young man?" he asked, pointing to Kevin. Kevin became angry. He felt the officer was accusing him because he was Black and Stephanie and Brett were White.

"Yes," the theft prevention officer said. "As a matter of fact, all three of them came in together. The lady was with them. The kid was seen by the store security putting CDs and videos in his pants, and he was observed removing the sensors and discarding them in different places in the store."

"This one pretended to fill out an application and began to ask me questions," the store manager said as he pointed to Kevin. "He and the lady were acting as lookouts for the kid."

Neither Stephanie nor Kevin could believe what was happening to them. Neither of them had any idea that Brett was stealing while they were in the store. Both of them tried to tell the store manager as well as the police officer that they did not know what Brett was doing.

"Hey, I just spent $35 of my money buying these CDs," Stephanie said. She tried to show the police officer what she had bought. She tried to show him her receipts. Of course, the police officer did not believe either Stephanie or Kevin. In the meantime,

Brett was trying to tell the men from the store that neither Stephanie nor Kevin knew what he was doing. He tried to tell them that they had nothing to do with his stealing. Because Brett was a minor, the police officer called his mother to the store.

When Brett and Stephanie's mother arrived, the officer allowed Brett to leave with her, but he arrested Kevin and Stephanie for shoplifting, which is a misdemeanor, and took them straight to jail. Kevin could not believe that the day that started with him giving his friend, Stephanie, and her 12-year-old brother a ride to the store would end with him being arrested for shoplifting. He did not understand why he and Stephanie went to jail and Brett went home. He could not understand why no one believed him when he said that he did not have anything to do with Brett stealing from the store, even after Brett admitted that he acted alone.

Little did he know that his being arrested was just the beginning of a nightmare that he would not wake up from any time soon. That day would be the end of life as he had known it before he picked up his friend, Stephanie, and her brother, Brett.

When they arrived at the police station, Kevin was booked in. He was fingerprinted, and his picture was taken. Then he was strip-searched and made to dress in the jail uniform—that ugly, dreaded, orange jumpsuit. He could not fathom how he ended up in jail. He was innocent. He did nothing wrong. After spending about 10 hours in jail, he was finally taken up to court to see a judge, who set a bond for him for $2,500. Kevin spent two nights in jail before his mother was able to come up with the money to get him out. It cost his mother $600 cash to get him out. Kevin felt bad because he knew that his mother was spending the rent money to get him out of jail.

Both Kevin and Stephanie had the same court date. They both pled not guilty. Kevin believed that when he and Stephanie told the judge and the prosecutor their side of the story, that everything would be okay. They were given another court date to come back. Kevin, Stephanie, Brett, along with his mother, showed up at court for the second court date. They were ready to tell the judge what really happened. Brett told the judge that neither Stephanie nor Kevin had anything to do with his stealing from the store. However, the witness from the store did not show up and the judge continued the case so that the witnesses from the store could be present even though Brett told him that Kevin and Stephanie were innocent.

The next time Kevin came to court, it was the trial date. This was his third time in court and he expected Brett and Stephanie to be there as they had in the past. He learned too late that Stephanie had a different trial date. This time, the witnesses from the store showed up and the judge forced him to go to trial WITHOUT the benefit of a lawyer and WITHOUT the benefit of his witnesses, especially Brett.

Kevin had what is called a bench trial; that is, the judge would be the only one to hear the evidence in the case and would decide if Kevin was guilty or not. The judge found Kevin guilty of shoplifting and put him on probation for 12 months. The case against Stephanie was dismissed. Brett's case was handled in juvenile court, and he never spent one night in jail—even though he had been caught shoplifting before.

Three years later, Kevin, as a 20 year old, found that because he had a record showing that he was convicted for shoplifting, he was unable to find a job that paid more than the minimum wage. He was branded a thief, and his conviction will be hard to overcome. But he knows that with time and perseverance, he can have a new beginning.

MORAL LESSON

Kevin should not have gone to court without a lawyer. He should have asked the judge for a lawyer and a jury trial. With a jury trial, Kevin would have had a chance to call Brett and Stephanie as witnesses and the jury would have decided if Kevin was innocent or guilty. Most importantly, Kevin learned too late, you can be arrested just because you are in the store with someone when that person steals merchandise from the store. If he had not left his car door unlocked, Brett would never have been able to place the stolen items in his car. Unfortunately, he was punished because he was with the person that stole and no one would believe him or Brett about what happened. He also realized that he didn't know as much about Brett and Stephanie as he thought. He would have been more careful had he known that Brett had shoplifted before.

CHAPTER

9

BEST FRIENDS

Lawanda Jean O'Bannon

*P*atrick Davis, known as Pat, and William Christian, known as Bill, were best friends. They met two years ago in 9th grade when they both started J.S. Abrams High School. They have been inseparable since then. Today was pickup day. They were headed to the courts in Midtown Park, where they would get in on a pickup basketball game. Everyone hung out there on Saturday afternoons, and if they were lucky, they would only have to wait about 45 minutes.

Pat was driving his mom's car, and Bill was on the passenger side. His mom had carpooled to work and left her car at home. Pat only had his driver's permit and was supposed to have a licensed driver in the car. However, he had taken his mom's car several times before and had never been stopped. And besides, if they were stopped, he would only get a traffic citation.

"Hey, Shorty," Bill said to Pat, using the handle he always used for him, "I need you to pull over at the corner store before we get to Midtown Park."

"Sure thing," Pat replied. As he pulled over to the parking area at the store, he noticed the neighborhood drug dealer, "Black," in the area. To his surprise, Bill got out of the car and headed straight towards Black. He was shocked when he saw them shake hands like old buddies. He didn't realize that Bill knew Black like that and that they were on speaking terms. He wondered to himself about several things: *What was Bill doing hanging out with Black? Was he selling drugs? Was he buying drugs?* This seriously disturbed him. After they spoke for several minutes, Bill came back to the car and said, "Let's go."

"What was that all about?" Pat asked. "When did you start hanging out with Black?"

Bill looked at him quickly and then looked away. "It's no big deal," he said. "It was nothing."

Pat bristled, "Man, don't tell me it was nothing! You know that guy sells drugs!" He was so excited that he didn't realize he had just run a red light. "Are you selling drugs for him?"

"Man, no; hell, no," Bill replied quickly and forcefully.

"Then you must be using!" Pat stated very pointedly. "Man, you know I'm not down with that! If you're doing drugs and hanging out with Black, you don't need to be riding with me. "Oooh, no ..."

Something in his tone made Bill pause and really look at him. "What?" he said, nervously looking at Pat.

"Man, the police are behind me," he stated as he slowed down to pull over. While he was occupied with stopping the car, he did not notice Bill take something out of his pocket and place it in the center console.

The officer approached on the driver's side and asked for his license and insurance. Pat sighed deeply and handed the officer his permit. The officer looked at the permit and then stooped low to peer in the car at Bill and asked, "Do you have a license?"

Of course, Bill said no. As the officer was looking at Bill, he noticed something in the console. When he focused his eyes on it more closely, he recognized what appeared to be marijuana in a clear plastic bag. "Alright, guys," he said, "I'm going to ask you to slowly place both hands on the dashboard and don't move." He motioned to his partner and said, "We have drugs in the car!"

"No, we don't!" Pat said incredulously.

"Well," the officer began, "what would you say that is in your console?"

Pat looked down, saw the drugs, and then looked at Bill. "Bill, what have you done?" he whispered.

Bill just shrugged his shoulders and looked away. He never said a word.

"Anybody want to own up to the drugs?" the officer asked.

Pat said, "They're not mine!"

Bill said nothing.

"OK, son, I need you to step out of the car and place your hands behind your back." The other officer was telling Bill the same thing. They were both being arrested for possession of drugs. Bill thought to himself, he was definitely getting more than a traffic citation this time. He wished he had listened to his mom when she told him not to drive without a licensed driver in the car, and he wished he had not allowed Bill to get back in his car after he met up with Black.

MORAL LESSON

Never succumb to peer pressure or hang out with someone who is doing drugs. Pat was arrested because he was the driver of the vehicle and denied that the drugs were his. Bill was arrested because he was present in a car that had drugs in plain view. The law presumes that any contraband, i.e., drugs, found in a car either belongs to the driver or the owner of the car. In this situation, because there were two people in the car and no one would own up to the drugs, the officer had the right to arrest both individuals and allow the court to sort it out. When drugs are in plain view for everyone to see, the law presumes that anyone present has constructive possession of the drugs and they can *all* be arrested.

CHAPTER
10

The Birthday Present

Lawanda Jean O'Bannon

Katie, short for Catherine, was a widowed mother raising two children in the city. Today was her day off, and it was such a lovely day. *Oh, I just love summertime,* she thought to herself. The sun was shining, the flowers were blooming, and today, it seemed like a thousand birds were chirping. "What a lovely day," she said out loud, as she stirred the brownie mix while looking out the kitchen window. She reached over and turned on the oven to let it preheat. Then she finished mixing the brownie batter, poured it into the prepared pan, and set it aside. "I'll wash everything up later," she said to herself.

As she poured her second cup of coffee, she thought of her two kids. Her oldest child had just turned seventeen a month ago and was working his first summer job. John was such a good kid, she mused to herself. He would be going into the 12th grade next year and then on to college. Janet was three years younger than John and would be starting high school next year. "Oh, my," she said, jumping at the sound of the doorbell ringing as she was startled out of her musings. She placed her coffee cup on the table and went to answer the door. She noticed a tall black guy, medium weight, wearing a brown suit with a county ID badge attached to his jacket standing there.

"May I help you?" she asked as she opened the door.

"Hi, my name is James White, and I am an investigator with the county police," he said as he handed her his business card. "Are you Ms. Smith, mother of John Smith?" he politely asked.

"Yes, I'm Mrs. Smith," she replied cautiously.

"Is your son at home?"

"No, he's not," she stated with much attitude as she placed her hands on her hips. "What is this about, sir?"

Now it was his turn to be cautious.

"Please forgive me for being so abrupt," he said apologetically. "I'm only here to conduct a preliminary investigation. May I come inside?" he asked nervously.

"Sure," she said, noticing his cautious deference to her stance. As she led him to the living room, she read his business card, which stated he was an investigator in the sex crimes unit of the County Police Department. "Please have a seat," she said as she waived her hand in the direction of the chair by the fireplace. "Now, what is this about?"

Placing his hands in front of him in a linked position and leaning forward, he stated, "Ma'am, your son has been accused of rape."

"What!?" she screamed. "What!?" she screamed again, jumping to her feet.

Mr. White, jumping up as well with his hands up and palms turned out trying to calm her, said in rapid succession, "Please, calm down! At this point, those are just allegations. He is not under arrest, and we are still investigating."

Pacing in a feverish manner, she replied rapidly as well, "When did this happen? Where did this happen? Who said it? Are you sure you have the right person?" The last question was almost a whimper.

"Well," he replied, "the young lady is fourteen years old, and she said it happened at a party one month ago. She said the party was at a house in the Sugar Hill community. She knows your son by name and face, and she described him in great detail. She said he forced her to have sex."

Looking him straight in the face, Mrs. Smith stated, "Sir, I don't know you. All I have to say is that you don't know my son, but I do. John would never, ever, do anything like that!!! For God's sake, he has a fourteen-year-old sister himself!!"

Taking a deep breath, Mr. White stated, "Well Ma'am, like I said, we are still investigating. I'm going to ask you to bring your son down to the station when he comes home." And with that he left.

Katie's mind was racing. *Oh my God! Not my son! He wouldn't do anything like this!* "John!! John!!" she screamed when she heard him come into the house. "How *could* you?" she screamed even louder.

"MOM, what is it?" John asked frantically.

"They said ... they said ..." She could hardly speak for breathing so hard. It seemed like she had been running forever and couldn't catch her breath. Finally she managed to say between breaths, "An officer came by here today and said that you had been accused of rape. That you forced a fourteen-year-old girl to have sex. He said it happened at a house in Sugar Hill one month ago. Is it true? Don't lie to me! Don't you dare lie to me!"

John looked at his mother as if he was seeing her for the first time. He stared so long that she began to fear that it was true. As he stared, he felt her fear; he saw the wrinkles in her face that were absent this morning; he noticed her wringing hands and the short breaths she was taking. But above all else, he saw something he had never seen before—absolute terror. He knew he could not lie to her. He would not lie to her. Very calmly, as if he was consoling a grieving mother who had just lost a child, he spoke in a gentle voice, showing strength way beyond his seventeen years and said, "It's not true, Mom." John continued saying, "Mom, I love you, and I love Janet, and I would never, ever, do anything to disrespect you or my lil' sister. I didn't rape anybody, and I didn't force anybody to have sex."

"Then what happened?" his Mom interjected. "Why would she lie? Didn't you know how old she was?"

Calmly again, John answered, "Mom, I don't know why she lied. I didn't know how old she was. She looked like she was my age, and she definitely looked older than Janet. Mom, you may not like what I'm about to say, but this is the truth about what happened. You remember last month was my birthday?"

His mother nodded yes. "Well, I went to a party in Sugar Hills with Fred and some other guys. When we got there, I met this girl I had seen before in the Sugar Hill area. She knew it was my birthday and said she had a present for me."

"What kind of present? I thought you said you didn't rape anybody?" she interjected again.

"Mom, will you listen?"

"OK," she replied, then said, "Hurry up and get to the point, sweetie. This is killing me."

"We went into a room ..." John continued "... after she said she had always liked me and wanted to show me how much. Mom, she performed oral sex on me. I didn't force her. We didn't even kiss. When she finished, we both went back to the party. I swear I didn't touch her."

"That's it?" his mom asked. "Is that all?"

"That's it, Mom, nothing else happened," he replied.

John, his mom, and Fred sat in the waiting area at the County Police Department. They were waiting for Investigator James White. When he came to the waiting room, he escorted them to a smaller room with a table and four chairs. John and his mom had decided to come to the station to give his version of what happened. She figured they had nothing to hide. Of course she had spoken with Fred, and he corroborated what John had told her and added that everybody at the party knew about it. She was so relieved that John had not had sex with the young girl and had reprimanded him for what he allowed to happen. But, boys will be boys. Nonetheless, she was confident that there would be no charges once John told what really happened.

When John finished talking, Investigator White asked John to stand up. When John stood up, he asked him to turn around and began handcuffing him. "What are you doing?" his mother demanded.

"I'm arresting your son," he replied.

"What for?! He told you he didn't rape her. She gave him oral sex. There was no force. So, what are you arresting him for?"

Investigator White looked at her and said, "Ma'am, your son just admitted to having oral sex with a fourteen-year-old girl, and that is a crime. He is being arrested for aggravated child molestation."

"But it was a birthday present," she wailed. "He didn't do anything," she said in bewilderment.

MORAL LESSON

Always consult with an attorney before giving any statements to the police or before allowing your kids to speak with the police. What may appear like harmless actions of minors may be criminal offenses in the eyes of the criminal justice system. Had John and his mom consulted an attorney, they would have learned that John, although seventeen, was viewed as an adult in the eyes of the criminal justice system and that he could be charged with child molestation. They would have learned that *any* sexual activity with a fourteen-year-old girl would be a crime, whether she initiated contact or not, because her consent to engage in such activities was immaterial. They would have learned that any form of sex with someone fifteen years or younger is a felony offense, punishable by mandatory jail time, if convicted, and mandatory registration as a sex offender.

A BOUT THE AUTHORS

Clara Hunter King

Clara began the practice of law as a Criminal Defense Attorney in November of 1996, and opened her own law firm in 1998. Prior to entering law school she owned and operated a paralegal firm. Her interest in the legal profession dates back to her childhood days of watching Perry Mason on television.

Yvonne Hawks

Yvonne is a Public Defender for the city of Atlanta. She began her practice in 1998.

She has always been fascinated with the practice of criminal law. She saw the practice of law as a way to help those caught up in the criminal justice system because she has learned that the system can be quite taxing, even for trained professionals.

Lawanda Jean O'Bannon

Lawanda began her practice as a Criminal Defense Attorney in 1996, and is currently a Senior Trial Attorney in the Fulton County Public Defender's office. She entered the legal profession because of her growing concern for the inadequate representation of young Black men.

Janine Brooks-Collier

Janine is a Private Investigator, and has been in the criminal justice community for over sixteen years. She began her career in law enforcement and has been a private investigator for ten years. She has investigated numerous criminal cases including high profile federal cases, as well as capital and felony murder cases. She has assisted attorneys not only in cases that have gone to trial, but in many that have resulted in acquittals for her clients.

Betty Williams-Kirby

Betty chose the legal profession because she saw this as an opportunity to be of service to the community. She began the practice of law after she graduated from John Marshall law school in 1997. Growing up in the 1960's motivated her to want to fight injustice.